A 1st Century Idea for a 21st Century Global Church

Joel Holm

ISBN: 0-9861819-9-4
ISBN-13: 978-0-9861819-9-3

DEDICATION

To my dad

◆ A little guidance from a wanderer

Thanks for taking time to read this small book. It's not a new theological teaching. My goal is to present an idea. It's not an original idea. It's actually quite an old idea. But it is one that needs a lot more attention today.

Here's the idea:

There is much debate as to what is the biggest problem in the world. The list ranges from global health issues to corrupt government leadership to the spiritual void of the world. All are serious issues but not the primary problem. When the primary problem is addressed, all these other issues will also be addressed.

The primary problem is that too many Christians have yet to give themselves for the world like Christ did. This problem is not new. Dynamic church leaders, instilling passion and providing opportunities, has not solved the problem. Individuals taking on a cause alone have not solved the problem.

The answer is in a different type of leadership identity and community.

We need a Christian community where the average Joe is the biggest influencer on the other average Joes. We need spiritual leadership that helps others' fulfill their visions.

This idea is not a criticism of today's church leaders.

Just as it did in the early church, the idea compliments, not contradicts, what already exists. God loves paradoxes and this is just one more. In a church that needs visionary leaders, it's the personal leader that will have the greatest influence. The more intimate and agenda-less the invitation to God's global purpose becomes, the greater the mass mobilization will be.

Thanks for reading this document. Don't worry about grammar or writing style. Don't read it as a biblical theology. Don't expect to find many strategic implications. Read it as a first century idea whose time has come again.

Any feedback from you will help me sort through what I'm supposed to do with this idea. Special thanks to Aaron Searles for helping me shape this document.

Joel

Introduction

In ways both subtle and profound, we live in a global village. Every day, even as the teeming masses of humanity upon it multiply, the planet shrinks. Economically, culturally and spiritually, Earth is becoming more and more a world with blurring borders.

Today, a robust Internet and advancing communications technology have made voice and video, data and "real time" collaboration -- once the stuff of science fiction -- into an everyday virtual reality. In the realm of face-to-face meetings, too, global interaction has become the norm. No one is surprised today when a business trip has at least one foreign country on the itinerary. Indeed, the Federal Aviation Administration estimates that by 2015 there will be 1 billion air travelers annually.

In this global village, events half a planet away can immediately impact us, the news and its ripples racing – and beating – the next sunrise or sunset. A market crisis in Hong Kong or fluctuations in Saudi Arabian oil production boils over on the trading floors of Wall Street; news of a developing Atlantic storm off the Azores triggers hurricane watches along the Florida coast; an electronic exchange of world currencies in Paris, London or Brussels suddenly shrinks the buying power of the dollar.

This instant cause-and-effect cycle rides on the backbone of the Internet, which in just two decades has gone from being an egghead oddity to comprising the universally accepted digital glue that binds the global village together.

Consider this: In 1984, there were believed to be 1,000 Internet capable devices; currently there are over 600 million, according to industry estimates.

By 2008, the popular social networking website, Facebook, boasted more than 120 million active users. Then there's Skype.com, which provides software that uses Internet connections to make free telephone, videoconferencing and instant messaging and file exchange contacts with others in its 200 million-strong, international network.

In areas that really matter, at the core of our existence – where and how we work, socialize, learn and even express our faith – we are increasingly intertwined, our associations rapidly expanding beyond national borders. Whether Americans, Europeans, Asians or Africans, we have all been grafted – willingly or not – into a planet-spanning, interdependent community.

And, that global village has adopted a universal language: English. India and China, the two most-populous nations on the face of the earth, both have adopted the tongue as their language for international trade: In India 100 percent of college graduates speak English, while studies indicate that within the next decade the Chinese will become the single largest English-speaking group in the world.

But in this melting pot of cultures, economies and ideas, where is the church? It is the question Christians must ask; the fate of billions – in this life, and in eternity – is at stake.

◆ Globalization: First Century Style

In a way, though, the church has been here before. For guidance in how to reach the developing global community for Christ in the 21st Century, we would do well to study how our spiritual forbearers did the same in the 1st Century.

Despite the passage of two millennia, the two periods have much in common. As Christ's followers exploded out of Jerusalem and into the expanses of the known world within a generation of the crucifixion, it was the Roman Empire – the very source of the faith's persecution – that also proved to be its catalyst for evangelism.

The Empire was at its peak in the 1st Century. Roman roads connected a realm that stretched from Spain, modern-day France and Germany in the west to Egypt, Syria and Arabia in the east. Roman shipping plied the Mediterranean; the image of Caesar appeared on coins used in commerce; and the Greek language was the common tongue in both the streets and the palaces of the Empire.

The early church used all those facets of Roman civilization to advance the Kingdom of God. It is time for the church of today to do the same in the new global village; to become the effective steward of the opportunities God is providing at this latest, critical crossroads of history. Not since the 1st Century has there been such a scenario of opportunity for all of God's Church to impact the world.

But if we are to truly release the Body of Christ we need a new breed of leader. More to the point, we need to identify these leaders, recognizing that they are already among us – but until now have lacked development or encouragement.

For example, consider Mark Mohr, the owner of a marketing firm in Chicago. Like many other Christians, Mark goes to church on Sundays and participates in a small men's fellowship group once a week. Nothing remarkable there, you say? But Mark was a dormant, new Kingdom leader, unknown to himself and others.

The change came after Mark and his wife took a trip to Nairobi, Kenya and experienced not only the global village – but the global church. They made lasting connections – both personal and technologically -- with their brothers and sisters in Kenya, and took a new zeal and purpose back with them to the United States.

Today, Mark offers his employees the chance to go to Africa and offer their expertise in business development within that continent's developing markets. Mark pays their air fares and gives them the time for the trips, without them having to use personal vacations. Having recognized his business acumen as an under-utilized avenue for ministry, he is working to similarly enlist other Christian business leaders.

How many other Marks are out there, attending services and church activities, yet still feeling there could be, there should be, something more?

♦ John the Baptist: An unrecognizable leader

John the Baptist likely is not the first – or even second, third or fourth – biblical example you would think of when considering the characteristics of the new breed of Christian leaders we need today. Certainly, he does not meet the standard Christian leadership model we have now.

Even in John's day, the spiritual authorities of the time were confused about exactly who and what he was. Instead of priestly robes, he wore a rough camel's hair garment.

John did not bother to claim fame as a prophet, and he had no messianic aspirations for himself. His identity was different but his influence was profound.

People flocked to the Jordan River to confess their sins and be dipped by John, while he spoke of being only the lowly servant of the Christ to come. He was satisfied to refer to himself simply as "a friend of the bride groom." His ministry, then, was defined not by who he was, but who the coming Christ would be to a world in the throes of spiritual death.

Like John the Baptist, today's new breed of Christian leaders may defy being easily pegged. Not defined – or limited – by traditional church leadership roles such as pastors, teachers, department leaders or deacons, the new Kingdom leader can be anyone and anywhere within the universal Body of Christ. In addition to paid ministers, they can be businessmen and businesswomen, teachers, factory workers, farmers, retirees, students and housewives, either recently saved or lifelong believers.

These leaders are not united by wealth, poverty, education or ordination, but by something far richer and profound: passion and love for Christ and His Church, and the willingness to see that Church transformed, one believer at a time. They are budding friends of the bridegroom.

Recently, I asked a group of pastors to write down the one thing that really gives them fulfillment. Every one of them identified some particular task or measure from their particular ministry gifting. Their answers were not wrong, but neither were they the answer given by John the Baptist:

"My joy is complete when I hear the bride groom's voice." To his or her personal, intimate relationship with Christ, the 21st Century Kingdom leader adds something distinct to our leadership model – a perspective that it is the Lord who strategically is the target audience.

Let me explain that further. Modern ministry can be a selfish place with self-serving agendas, founded on an equation that focuses on the ministry's leader, its followers and their common goals – growth in numbers, outreach programs or bigger church facilities, for example. It becomes about the work, and successful conclusions. This is not wrong.

Yet, too often, that's where leadership in the church today ends. John the Baptist avoided defining his ministry solely by task, but, as a friend to the bridegroom, enlisted himself in the complete vision of what God was doing. Even after he had preached about the coming Messiah, and then baptized him, John's passion for the Kingdom of God did not wane.

Sitting in Herod's prison, he still remained involved.

John sent messengers to Jesus with questions. He wanted reassurance that Jesus was indeed the Promised One. John continued to take his responsibilities as a leader in God's plan seriously; even as he approached the end of his own life by the headsman's ax, he was immersed in heaven's agenda, not his own.

Friend of the bridegroom leaders are dedicated to seeing the universal Body of Christ grow and become all it can be.

Once, their intent is recognized, such leaders quickly win trust from others. Like John the Baptist, their commitment and purpose extends to seeing everyone move forward in their own unique service in God's Kingdom.

When the religious leaders of his world demanded John identify himself and his ministry, his simple answer was "I am the voice." A voice does not fulfill a task; it does not see visions become reality; it is more than a message or decibels. A Kingdom leader's voice is not measured by direct accomplishment but its ability to influence others.

When we discover our voice, in whatever arena it resides, we also discover genuine humility. In other words, we find the person God truly created us to be.

When John the Baptist said he was not even worthy to untie the coming Messiah's sandals, he was not being especially humble. Rather, he was secure in knowing who he was – and was not. Our new Kingdom leaders will have this same attitude, accepting that there likely will be little recognition from others for their service. Their target audience will be Jesus himself.

♦ It's not what we know, it's who we trust

Human history is replete with examples of that truth.

We knew the world was flat. Wrong. OK, then, the sun revolves around the earth. Wrong, it's the other way around. Fine, but we certainly knew that when a person is ill, they need a good bleeding – open a vein, or pile on the leeches! Oops, wrong again. Well surely, it is obvious that certain races are more intelligent, created superior to others.

Oh boy. Really wrong.

Even some of our heroes of faith got it wrong on occasion. Old Testament scripture tells us that the prophet Samuel knew the king of Israel had to be that fine, strapping handsome man, Saul. Then when Saul went astray, Samuel learned that God's chosen successor was not the most obvious of Jesse's brood of sons, but the youngest one – a ruddy kid who had to be called out of the fields from watching the sheep in order to be anointed.

Elijah, having fled to a cave, thought he was the only man in Israel still faithful to God. He wanted to just die, a failure in his own mind. God had to remind him that Elijah knew nothing, that He had preserved thousands who had remained true.

Even Jesus' disciples thought they knew how the Messiah should act. So they chased little children away from him – only to be chastised as the Lord welcomed the tots to his embrace and blessing.

One of those disciples, Peter, later was convinced he knew how the church should relate to the new Gentile believers. It took a rooftop nap and a startling vision to show him God had decreed Jews and Gentiles alike worthy of his Son's love, sacrifice and salvation.
It was what these leaders thought they knew that got in the way of God's Kingdom, and temporarily crippled their own service to him. It is the same today, and the warning of Proverbs 3:5 remains as fresh now as when Solomon penned the words some 3,000 years ago : "Do not lean on your own understanding."

So, just what is it that we think we know about being a Christian in the 21st Century? How do those perceptions shape leadership – and limit what God wants to do through us?

In the New Testament church, similar questions needed answering. What developed was a leadership taking root in a world that was both culturally diverse and far-flung and yet bound by the Roman Empire's roads, laws and a shared language.

Now, history echoes those same crossroads through 21st Century parallels of those ancient connections: technology expressed in intercontinental travel and instant communications, intertwining economics, a shared proficiency in English and perhaps the most critical and universal factor of all – the need for God's love and grace.

Likewise, today there also is the need for those distinct early church leadership voices that will shape how Christ followers life out their faith within our global and to each human life in it.

What follows are illustrations of such leadership voices from the pages of the New Testament, as well as our own era. It is important to see these as examples of new Kingdom leadership identities, not a list of roles. Please note, too, I am not suggesting we no longer need or want our more traditional leadership methods or styles. What I do propose, though, is that the 1st Century leadership voices that rather quickly propelled an obscure Jewish sect into a life-changing faith embraced by millions must now re-emerge – if we are to reach our own time's billions.

♦ Barnabas: The Connector

Ephesians 4 teaches us that without unity we cannot become mature and attain to the whole measure of the fullness of Christ. Like when Paul wrote that more than 19 centuries ago, his spiritual offspring of today need a new voice of unity.

As a pre-converted Saul, the author of Ephesians was a zealous persecutor of the church. He was the bloody-handed foe of believers; his actions brought imprisonment and death to unknown numbers of early Christians. So, his sudden, dramatic conversion to the faith he had once so loathed understandably was met with fearful skepticism by church leaders of the time.

But God helped Barnabas see beyond the man who had been Saul, to glimpse the apostle who would be Paul. It was Barnabas who acted, bringing Paul to meet with church leaders – to join the hands of former adversaries in a clasp of future brotherhood. (Acts 9:26)

Barnabas had nothing to gain from this, and his was not a role that fit into any ecclesiastical organization chart. Indeed, he undertook a mission that brought great risk to his personal safety, his ministry and the trust others in the church had for him. Barnabas did all this because he knew the Kingdom of God flourished only in unity, and unity's foundation is built on connection.

Yes, connection. Could it be that what we think of as being the key ingredient of unity – a sort of universal submission and agreement that brooks no debate -- is wrong? Once we truly connect, we may continue to disagree on many things; it is that divine connection, though, that will transform our purpose and commitment.

Consider this: Most problems Christians and churches face fall within four areas: spiritual, leadership, strategic and relational. Regardless the specifics, our problems will be comprised of issues within one, several or even all of these categories. Most often, though, it is the relational piece that comes to the forefront – and the bitter irony is that this also is the area least addressed today. Numerous resources and program ideas address issues related to leadership development, strategic planning and personal spiritual formation. There are far fewer aids related to getting Christians and churches connected relationally.

Churches that are self-absorbed may manage numerous outreach programs, but they will not have a relationship with lost people. Churches that are isolated do not have a relationship with other churches. Christians that are oblivious to the world's suffering have no relational connection to people in those regions. And, churches that cling to the narrow-minded attitudes of the past do not have relationships with the diverse parts of the global Body of Christ.

Have a family spend two weeks with an undocumented immigrant dad, mom and their seven-year old daughter and that family may come out of the experience with a different perspective – and appreciation – for the immigration issue.

Compassion takes place through connection. That's why God sent his son to step out of time and eternity and into human flesh.

When a congregation gets connected to a poverty-stricken church in Africa, they change their perspective on budgets. When a church gets related to another fellowship in town, they change their perspective on territorialism.

The voice of unity does not try to bring agreement among churches, but connection. Only when we are connected — locally, regionally and globally, in a truly Kingdom way — will we begin to collaborate and contribute together, with each partner using its gifts and callings to bless the whole.

This is where the new kind of Christian leader, the Connector, will be crucial. This kind of leader, perhaps unrecognized by his or her fellows, but beloved of God — will thrive and see the church transformed, as it fulfills God's vision for His kingdom.

Our ministries today are built around trying to get people to contribute. We expend our energy, money and creativity in recruit workers to the cause. But if we don't first address the need for connection and collaboration, we will always struggle with contribution. This is what Barnabas understood; that everybody has a role to play in God's vision -- and that without genuine connection and collaboration, the unity needed to fulfill that vision would be stillborn.

♦ Sharon: A New Zealand housewife

Meet Sharon, a typical, middle-aged housewife in Whangerei, New Zealand – and one of this new breed of Kingdom leaders were discussing. Seeing the more than 30

churches in her community self-isolated in their own outreaches, Sharon understood the need for connection and acted. Through her organizational and relationship-nurturing efforts, these diverse fellowships came together to celebrate what God is doing through each church not just in their city and nation, but globally.

That initial collaboration created an event where each of the churches set up informational displays and shared information and passion for their unique ministries. That event was a catalyst for relationships and collaboration.

These churches do not compete with each other. They value their distinct cause in the world. They worship together.

And the spark for all of this was Sharon seeing the need for true connection where there had been none before. She acted, investing the time to broker relationships – first one-on-one, then between church leaders and their congregations. As a result, those differing fellowships today actively explore ways they can collaborate within their neighborhood of the global village.

Too often, leaders in the Kingdom of God today are willing to make connections for the sake of their own ministries, but avoid making the same effort for the vision of others. So, what connections are formed within the Body of Christ are usually limited to people who already share common, comfortable ground.

But the kind of connection we need – the foundations upon which the early church depended, and people like Barnabas and Sharon facilitated – seldom begins in comfort.

The Bible tells us that "iron sharpens iron" and that does not happen without some sparks flying. In bringing Paul together with the leaders of the early church, Barnabas was joining former adversaries.

Only a leader – a connector – without his or her own agenda can be such a catalyst. Often, that means risking much to fulfill the visions of others by bridging the chasms between potential foes.

♦ A Jerusalem Conference in Bhutan

Bhutan, a south Asian kingdom wedged between China, India and Tibet, is an ancient, predominantly Buddhist and until recently, remote and isolated country. The Christian church here is small in numbers and under the fist of great persecution. Foreign ministry involvement is rare, so native believers are extremely protective of their connections outside Bhutan's borders.

That protective attitude even extends to other Bhutanese Christians, leaving the struggling national church fractured, and its leaders – though polite in public – cynical and weary of each other in private. It is common to hear each of these scattered Bhutanese Christian leaders comment on their particular ministry as the only real work being done, and few of them will share information on their "foreign partners."

In other words, for the struggling, isolated churches in Bhutan, the concept of unity was as elusive as the legendary yeti, or "abominable snowman" the folk of the Himalayas have recounted in fireside stories for untold generations.

Enter Ron, an Indian Christian with ministry interests in Bhutan. For several years, Ron had worked with one particular network in developing a church-planting strategy for Bhutan; he invested his time and money, building ministry in the country.

But Ron could see that much more was needed if the gospel was to thrive in Bhutan. Connections, relationships and collaboration were missing – and unity was nonexistent. So, when one leader, a friend of Ron's, offered to host a two-day gathering of Bhutanese

Christians, Ron took the first small step toward forging true connection; he shook things up by insisting that a different leader host the second day.

"I wanted to feel the awkward tension when I walk in the room," Ron recalled. And, that is how it began, too. For two days these Bhutanese church leaders met, stiffly formal with each other at first, but then gradually more open and honest in their exchanges. As understanding and trust grew, the seeds of unity were sown; the gathering ended in a time of fervent prayer for each other.

It was a first, but big step for which Ron risked much.

The whole thing easily could have ended with the same distance and distrust with which it began, perhaps leaving the Bhutanese church even more at odds. It would have been much easier for Ron to simply continue working with just one of the groups rather than risk failure and further segregation of these Bhutanese Christian bodies -- not to mention the possible unraveling of his own work and reputation.

Ephesians 4 shows us that God's design is for everyone to contribute to the creation of His Kingdom on Earth, and in the 21st Century we have the opportunity and means to work together as we never have before. To do that, though, we need a spiritual paradigm shift; we need to get our focus off getting others to contribute to our vision, and together share in building His vision.

Ron, like Barnabas, chose the path of the Connector, helping transform that one corner of the Kingdom through building relationships.

♦ Philip: The Inviter

In most of our churches today, leaders look out over their congregations and assign the people in them to two groups using the so-called "80/20" principle. The axiom accepted by so many pastors is that 80 percent of the work is done by 20 percent of the people – and 80 percent of the money, too, is given by the same 20 percent.

But why should that be etched in stone? Couldn't it be just as well the "50/20/20/10" principle or the

"5/5/5/5/5/5/5/5/5...you get the idea" principle? Why should we blindly accept that Christians are fated to forever fall within two groups -- one engaged if the work, life and giving of the church, and one on the sidelines looking on?

The 21st Century church needs leaders who see not groups but individuals, and understands that each one needs a personal invitation to be immersed within what God wants to accomplish in and through them. Carrying that thought further, perhaps truly becoming a bigger church means getting tighter and multiplied and especially more intimate.

The Great Barrier Reef, stretching some 1,600 miles off the coast of Australia, is a living organism visible from space. But it consists of 2,900 individual reefs and 900 coral islands literally made up of billions of tiny creatures called coral polyps. Out of the many, nature has formed the world's biggest single, living structure, one that in turn creates a massive ecosystem teeming with sea life.

The global church must be the spiritual equivalent of that natural wonder. The Great Barrier Reef has a common, unifying bond – life. So, too, the Internet has no CEO or centralized headquarters, yet hundreds of millions of people are connected to each other and thus unified in a decentralized way.

A decentralized Body of Christ, united by its devotion to the gospel, should strive to form intimate connections. Our identity comes from our personal relationships with Christ and each other. Everyone in the body needs to be invited; every individual needs an inviter . . . and that is another characteristic of the new Kingdom leader.

Jesus invited Phillip, a disciple of John the Baptist and a friend of fellow fishermen Peter and Andrew. Phillip also, it is thought, had connections with the Greek-speaking members of the community – and scripture notes it was Phillip who brought gentiles to meet with Jesus.

When the Lord called Phillip he did not tell him to do anything else but follow him. But Phillip immediately found Nathaniel with his excitement over the rabbi he believed was the Messiah, Jesus of Nazareth. Nathaniel's initial reaction was not very promising; he ridiculed Phillip by smirking, "Can anything good come out of Nazareth?"

But because Phillip is a leader, he persists. Come and see for yourself, he says. Come and experience Jesus, personally.

He invited me, and I now invite you. The result? A changed life for a despised tax collector who would, along with those of the other apostles, bring the message of peace to the world.

An Inviter. This is not a ministry role that appears on the bylaws and constitutions of a church or denomination. It is, however, an essential role because everyone needs to be first invited before a meeting can take place, a relationship established, collaboration realized and a global village reached for Christ.

The leader who personally invites is the church's voice of intimacy. Too often when churches want people to participate, the invitation is markedly impersonal, addressed to a large group – and woefully ineffective. The individual, lost in a faceless mass of humanity, hears no personal invitation; he only hears a recruiting message.

Phillip did not recruit Nathaniel. His appeal was personal, one that conveyed excitement and an invitation to "come and check this out for yourself." That was both the simplicity, and the power of his invitation, that it was delivered one-on-one.

During one of my flights the airline asked passengers to complete a survey rating the service they had received. If some faceless voice had come over the public address system with the request, I never would have bothered. But an airline representative personally approached me. The head purser came to my seat, addressed me by name, shook my hand and asked me if I would fill out the survey questionnaire. I responded by doing so.

Unlike the purser, Phillip had no agenda except for Nathaniel's good; still, this story of mine illustrates the value of a personal invitation, even at its most basic expression, to shape people's attitudes and actions.

♦ Mike: A 'no-agenda' inviter

Mike, the missions director at Pastor Rick Warren's Saddleback Church, has an enormous job in his own right.

But Mike is also one of the new breed, global Christian leaders who saw the need to connect with other mission pastors. He made it a point to personally invite those colleagues to a gathering held informally every six months or so.

He did not create a network, and he was not recruiting anyone to participate in Saddleback's own extensive missions programs. He was not some "expert" calling a conference aimed at raking in support or dollars. No, Mike was one of them, with no agenda but to bring these leaders together; he knew that from such connections come relationships, and from such relationships, collaborative ministries could grow.

Without Mike's personal invitation, many of these leaders would not have bothered to attend. But because Mike took the time to make a few phone calls and send some emails, something was born that continues to grow in its influence on countless lives through the ministries of many leaders.

Phillip asked Nathaniel simply to "come and see." Hey, pal, I invite to you just take that one step. Just do this one thing and see what might happen.

One step, as it turns out, is always how a journey begins.

And for most of us, to take a step off the path we blindly are following, we need the power of a personal invitation like Phillip's – or Mike's. We need a new breed of leader not afraid or too busy to initiate personal invitations to people to move just one step forward in their own story with God.

These invitations should extend beyond just the Christian family, though. I know of a church in England that decided to renovate a public school as a community outreach. Members worked hard and did a beautiful job, enlisting hundreds of their own people to participate in the project. They won the gratitude of the neighborhood they had blessed; but they missed out on an even greater opportunity.

This church showed a great heart in this project, but they failed to invite the community itself to be part of the work – part of the journey. There were no invitations to the parents of the children who would attend the refurbished school nor to other civic or business leaders to join with them.

As wonderful as the project was, what future collaboration – and opportunity for the gospel – may have been created by inviting everyone to participate, regardless of where they were with their own journeys of faith?

♦ James: The Confirmer

Can doubt be part of ministry? It was with Nathaniel, who scoffed at the possibility of something good having come out of a little hick town like Nazareth. But Nathaniel, personally invited by Phillip, took that first step – and that made all the difference.

In the global church, everyone needs to be involved, personally invited to their calling, and it is inevitable that doubts will come. We will doubt our actions, our plans, our capabilities – even our understanding of God's calling on our lives.

The New Kingdom Leader also must have the characteristic of a confirmer. I believe all Christians have callings, but many are prevented by doubts and fears from acting on them. Spiritually paralyzed, they desperately need a new kind of leader to step into their lives with the voice of confidence.

Oh, we ministers have the exhorting part of ministry down well enough: "You can do anything through Jesus," we declare. But we need leaders who personally confirm to a self-doubting Christian that "This is the thing Jesus would have you do!"

In the 1st Century church, such a leader was James.

When a major controversy arose over Paul and Barnabas taking the gospel to the Gentiles, debate raged. Was it right to take what had begun as Christ's message to the children of Israel and give it to non-Jews? If so, how are they saved?

Should they follow the laws we were raised with? Should they be circumcised as we have been? Have Paul and Barnabas gone too far?

And so a conference was convened. Paul and Barnabas testified to what they had experienced, how the gentiles were just as hungry and responsive to the Good News about Jesus as many of their Jewish brethren had been.

Many in that meeting did not agree. James waited for things to calm down, and then he stood up and made a strong leadership declaration.

"Listen to me," he said. James, with a voice of confirmation, sealed what God was already speaking to their hearts. He reminded them of Peter's own testimony about gentiles accepting the Lord, and proclaimed that if they needed more evidence of this universal salvation, Paul and Barnabas had provided it. James confirmed that gentile conversions were a fact – and that now requiring them to follow Jewish traditions amounted to questioning the work of the Holy Spirit.

Into what could have been a destructive debate James spoke with confidence in what God was doing. The doubts of the early church were eased, and the faith went on to spread like wildfire through the known world. At a critical moment, a confirmer had stepped into the fray.

Our rapidly changing world requires a church not afraid to change its ways of doing things, even as it keeps the message of Christ pure and current. If we're to reach this world, in addition to our traditional ministry roles of pastors, evangelists, missionaries and teachers, we need to adopt an attitude of the ordination of all the vocations Christians represent. Everyone has a role in God's Kingdom work. This will take radical action on the part of each believer that will be filled with its share of doubts and fears, needing a personal leader confirming, "This is Jesus' plan for you."

♦ Revisiting Mark's story

Remember Mark Mohr, mentioned at the beginning of this document? He is a good example of someone with a non-traditional ministerial vocation, in this case that of a businessman, whose gifting should be welcomed into the family of ministries ordained of God.

When that trip to Africa stirred his desire to go beyond the comfort zone of church attendance and tithing and onto personal ministry to the global church, Mark did not quit his job and become a missionary; he did not even join his local church's missions team. Instead, he re-evaluated his role as a business leader – and his responsibility to the 67 of his 70 employees who were not saved.

Over the next three years Mark's life turned upside down. His corporate goals changed as he measured his life differently. There were doubts and fears about this uncharted course at every turn, but Mark was not alone in making this transition from a business owner and good Christian man into a faith-filled believer living out his calling through business.

God spiritually parachuted two new breed of leaders into Mark's life who spoke to him with confidence and confirmation. They challenged him, encouraged him, reminded him who God was, and that He could be trusted.

They did not try to recruit him to their cause but moved him to God's cause for his life.

Confirmers know that Jesus will never let those called according to His purpose fail. They are not prophets. They are not experts. They confirm who Jesus is and what He already is speaking to the heart of a Christian. And, confirmers know the alternative to action is to do nothing and stagnate into ineffectiveness. These are the new breed of leader who is not important by his or her title, but by the confident words they speak when doubts and fear arise.

People will often forget the exact words of a confirmer but they will always remember how they felt in their presence – and how that boost of confidence at a critical moment spurred them to take the next step.

♦ Nathan: Releasing marketplace ministers

Nathan has served churches in the Arab world for more than two decades, but a few years ago he had the idea of seeing Christian businessmen use their resources and expertise for more than just funding ministries. Nathan wanted to see them become ministers within their own arenas, the marketplaces of the Middle East.

So, he put together a gathering of key business leaders and their pastors to discuss the idea of forming Kingdom businesses. How, they were asked, could Arab churches and pastors embrace this idea and apply it to their churches? It was a new, radical departure from the ministry norm, and along with the interest and intrigue came an abundance of fear and cynicism.

The questions came like the pounding of rain on a tin roof. Would the church lose money in backing such enterprises? Could the business leaders themselves be sure of their spiritual qualifications for such ministry? Still, in the end, these same pastors and business leaders moved ahead with the plan.

Why? Because Nathan was a confirmer. He spoke confidence into the enterprise and acted as a catalyst for trust in God's blessing on this bold effort. He knew that God is a communicator, and that he had long ago planted the seed of this idea in the hearts and minds of these men. It was Nathan's role, at the appropriate time, to give that idea the form of words and direction. In doing so, he confirmed what these leaders had already sensed – and that gave them the boost they needed to act.

♦ Timothy: The Guide

We all need help, and we all can play a part in meeting the needs of others. In a nutshell, that summarizes what Paul told early Christians about how they would stand out – by their love for each other.

That means if I am a new breed of leader, I am devoted to doing anything I can to help others advance in their callings. I don't do it just because I'm bighearted; I do it because I'm called to a Kingdom. I do it because it's my calling and their ministry is my ministry. In this case, another characteristic of our new breed of Christian leader is that of being a guide.

When the church at Philippi needed direction, Paul had just the right young man for the job: Timothy. In Philippians 2:20 the apostle put it this way: ". . . I have no one like him, who will be genuinely concerned for your welfare." Timothy's interests were not in his own ministry, but in those of the people he went to lead.

This was a guide-leader whose heart for Christ was big enough to pulse beyond the boundaries of his own ministry; it is the same heart that needs to beat in the chests of the new kinds of ministers we must have to reach our global community.

The ministry of Timothy of the 21st Century will depended on the principle of influence stewardship. We all know about the importance of being good stewards of time and resources, but in the global church developing today, the resource of influence may be even more important.

God has given us an influence within our circles of friends, colleagues and business associates, and He calls us to wisely use that influence for His Kingdom. Along with measuring out our time, talent and money in His service, we need to take responsibility for guiding others into their own gifting and Kingdom opportunities.

Timothy knew the problems facing the church in Philippi, a new work struggling with the challenges of achieving unity by following Christ's example in putting the needs of others first. These were not Timothy's problems, but he took responsibility for them anyway. As a new breed of leader, Timothy took responsibility for problems he did not create, that were not his fault. He offered help to those who maybe were not even looking for help.

As a new breed of leader, Timothy followed the model of Jesus, who took responsibility for our sins and helped us even when we were not looking for help. Timothy got all that. We need to do so, too.

When I was pastoring a church it seemed everyone wanted something from me, regardless of whether they were from within or outside my congregation. Every week, the mail would bring multiple letters from ministries seeking financial support. Never, not once, did I receive a letter from one of these ministries offering support to our vision, or encouragement to build us up in tough times.

When I started working in ministry outside of the church I made it a point to open each conversation with a pastor by saying, "I'm not looking for a place to preach and I don't want any money from you. I think I can help you, no strings attached." These pastors would be speechless – utterly amazed that someone actually took an interest in their church and in their vision.

When I tell this story, inevitably among the first questions I get from Christian leaders goes like this: "How did you take care of yourself, then?" I always wondered why this was the first question asked.

It's not that the new Kingdom leader does not have his own vision and ministry with its own needs. But he is willing to make room for others' visions and needs even sacrificing his own fruitfulness to bless others, always keeping in the forefront the needs of the Kingdom.

When we have a movement of such leaders -- those who care first about others and understand the stewardship of influence -- the global church will awaken and be transformed into one unified in purpose, blessed by its diversity of ministries and gifts, and capable of participating in God's vision for a healthy, vibrant Body of Christ.

♦ David: So-called retired businessman

This David is a husband, a father and a retired owner of a successful business. But at the time in life when David's colleagues were taking it easy and enjoying the hard-won fruits of their labor, David and his wife, Pamela, began to get involved in business ministry ventures in Africa and Asia.

Shortly after initiating his Kingdom business ministry David met other business leaders – many of them young entrepreneurs – who expressed the desire to serve the Lord through their market and financial savvy. David was intrigued and offered himself as a mentor. He took on the mantle of coach and guide, helping these Christian colleagues achieve their dreams. He journeyed with them, their visions becoming his own.

Like Timothy, David desired to look beyond his own ministry to genuinely care and help empower the ministries of others – to use the experience of a successful business life to serve as a guide.

Today, David and Pamela thrive in that role, helping other Christian business leaders identify how their ministry as business leaders can impact nations. Recently, David took three young businessmen to China and Africa, introducing them to their counterparts there in a joint effort to develop micro-enterprises that could offer both jobs and hope to their countrymen.

◆ Matthew: The Preparer

One of the ongoing tensions in the lives of churches and individual believers alike is how they relate to the world at large. As many churches as exist, there are as many different answers to what that relationship should be.

But the new breed of Christian leader understands a simple, yet profound truth: In the global community, the engaged church must be part of the world – and the concerns of the world part of the church. The religious lines that formerly divided the church from the world in which it exists have already blurred and should be erased.

Religion has mixed with politics in ways both good and bad. Education, media, family and other arenas of society are integrated with spirituality. Faith is no longer merely private, but a public proposition in so many ways. These developments have opened opportunities for yet another Kingdom ministry, that of the Preparer.

We have long heard about the need to mobilize the church to reach the world, but what if what we think we know is wrong. What if it's more important that we mobilize the world for the church! That is exactly what Jesus taught his disciples to do in Luke 10, when he sent them out, two by two, as advance teams for his coming visits.

These disciples were mobilizing their world for Christ; to meet the spiritual hunger of the global community of the 21st Century, we will also need a corps of new Kingdom preparers.

The Apostle Matthew is the New Testament's prototype for this sort of ministry. In Luke 5, we first hear of Matthew the tax collector being called by Jesus. What was the next thing he did? Matthew threw a party for his new Master, and invited all his tax collector friends – disdained as among the worst of sinners -- to meet the Lord and his other disciples.

Matthew immediately discovered his gifting as a preparer. He created an environment where his friends could comfortably meet Jesus – where sinners could be prepared for relationship with their savior.

This is another example of the kind of leader the global church will need, and making room for such will require some major rethinking on our parts.

We wrongly distinguish between leading Christians inside the church and evangelizing those outside the church.

Christian leaders are for the church while Christian evangelists are for the world. But the 21st Century leadership model does not begin after conversion; it recognizes that God intended the church to lead the world – to provide guidance and inspiration to those outside the church.

It is this new breed of leader that is in the world, preparing his or her world to be reconciled to Christ. This is the voice of true community, and one that models Jesus' relationship with sinners.

This voice will speak through the mouths, ideas and actions of our new breed of Kingdom leaders, men and women ready to prepare the world to meet Jesus. In this developing global community of ours, marketplace leaders especially have been strategically positioned by God to lead the world, preparing it for Christ and His church.

♦ One more Dave: He led his world

This Dave, also a businessman, recognized some people in his church were victims of economic injustice. They lived paycheck-to-paycheck when they could, and had to rely on storefront "payday loan" company – with their outrageous interest demands -- when they could not. It is a trap low-income people become regularly ensnared by, a financial stranglehold that relies on their lack of financial sophistication.

Dave led both his church and his community by organizing financial education and service fair days. He convinced banks to provide financial planners at no cost.

He recruited corporate sponsorship. The ministries of his church provided all childcare, along with ushers and greeters to make the people feel welcome.

Dave's church did not create a financial services ministry just for its own people, but followed Dave's lead by inviting other members of their community to join in helping care for the community together. In the wake of these efforts, Dave was invited to sit on a major committee of city government. Another non-religious, not-for-profit in the city sought Dave's help in building bridges of collaboration to people of faith.

This church in the Pacific Northwest did not have to make a missions trip to serve the global community because its needs were in full view in its own backyard. Mobilized with the help of Dave, this fellowship responded to a pain that already existed among its own members – and reached out to the community at large, too.

You cannot lead the world if you're not part of that world.

David led his world. He prepared his village for the ministry of Christ.

♦ Preparing the world through love

A major flashpoint for this new breed of leader in carrying the banner of a global church into a developing global village could very well be Africa. He and she sees and responds to the scourge of AIDS, which the United Nations estimates has infected nearly 25 million Africans and killed more than 2 million, while leaving millions more children as orphans.

For this new breed of leader , this virus and the devastation it is wreaking amount to more than just another ministry opportunity; it is personal. In the faces of those enduring the ravishes of this killer disease, in the eyes of widows and the motherless, he sees his neighbor, his sister, his child. She is part of a community seeking to provide medicines to the sick, homes and education to the orphaned, and comfort to the dying and grieving.

Like Matthew, this new breed of leader is preparing his suffering corner of the world for the love, touch and saving grace of Jesus.

To this new Kingdom minister it is about much more than enlisting Christians in the latest community service projects, as valuable as those may be. She is a leader in her community – the guiding hand, the encouraging word, and the mentoring spirit of Christ's expressed through her passion, knowledge, experience and faith to act.

The leader sees his role playing out as much in the world – perhaps even more so – than within the boundaries of church walls or organization.

One church grasped the concept of global community and the global church with both hands, challenging its members to be that new breed of leader as a preparer in their community. They responded by joining school boards, volunteer fire departments, civic groups, taking any opportunity within their community to lead.

Not only did they see many of the people they influenced eventually come to personal relationships with Christ, but they transformed how their church saw itself – and how its community viewed the church.

"The local church is the hope of the world," says Willow Creek Community Church founder Bill Hybels. That profound truth is echoed through ministries worldwide today. But the reverse is also true: "The world is God's hope for the 21st century church."

We must not come to our world as a messiah. Our world already has the Messiah. The truth is we need the world because it takes a lost world to build a strong church! Why?

Because without a cause, the church always just plods along; with a cause, we thrive. Everyone needs to discover a personal cause. To do this, they need a new breed of leader.

It is this 21st century, globalized world that provides the best environment for us to live out our calling as a new breed of leader! From connecting to inviting and by confirming, guiding and preparing, this new, unfettered leadership – our new generation of leaders – could see church as we know it transformed. Like the church of the 1st Century, we, too, could see our world turned upside down for Christ.

♦ Where the leader grows

The idea of 1st century leadership modeled by Barnabas, James and John the Baptist is not new, but it is foreign to most experiences. Connector. Inviter. Confirmer. Guide.

Confirmer. Voice. These are not power words. Yet these leaders have the potential to influence in ways few can and will. But where do these leaders come from? How are they raised and released into their ministry. Here's the twist: You cannot manufacture these roles. You can't even recruit people to this leadership role. It is possible to recruit people to get volunteers, but they will not invite and connect they will only enlist. You can mobilize people to cheerlead your cause, but they will not confirm and guide, they will only promote. You can enroll people to serve in outreach projects, but they will not prepare and lead their world.

You cannot create a new breed of leader. However you can create an environment where leaders like Barnabas, Matthew and James can flourish. Like the Great Barrier Reef, there needs to be an ecosystem that allows these leaders to thrive. This ecosystem was evident in the early church. The 21st century provides a unique opportunity to create this spiritual ecosystem – a global Kingdom ecosystem.

What is a global Kingdom ecosystem? It's characterized by a global awareness and is teeming with life through relationships with diverse people and parts of the Body of Christ. This ecosystem has an identity grander than any single ministry organization, while celebrating the uniqueness of each living organism in it. Its life and health is measured by each individual contribution to the complete ecosystem.

This global Kingdom ecosystem can take form anywhere. Spiritual ecosystems from when local churches encourage members to discover their calling above and beyond departmental tasks. They take root when families develop connections to communities in the world. Life abounds when marketplace leaders develop strategic relationships for Kingdom causes.

God's Kingdom ecosystem grows wherever there is a voice, producing personal engagement with God's global cause. A thriving Kingdom ecosystem causes more new breed of leaders to come to life and prosper.

♦ Mature life flourishes in a healthy ecosystem

The development of these leaders into a Kingdom ecosystem can't be isolated from their spiritual growth. The more I'm a part of God's global Kingdom the more I grow in my relationship with Christ.

As a Christ-centered believer, I remain committed to my church but I'm not dependent on it. The church's programs don't serve me as they did when I was a new believer. My wife and I are mature Christians and already connected to other Christian couples, so we don't need a small group ministry to facilitate our growth.

We are already reaching our community, so we don't need serving opportunities through our church. We study the Word, and although it is always good to be taught from it, we don't need intense courses to facilitate our learning.

We are self-feeders. We're Christ-centered believers. We tithe not because we're sold out to our church's vision but because we are obedient to God's word – the same motivation we have to regularly attending church services.

We grew into Christ-centered believers, not after taking enough of the right courses, attending the right church and joining the right group. Within us, there is this new breed of leader ready to break out. We became Christ-centered when we were influenced by a new breed of leader in a Kingdom ecosystem that connected us to God's global cause.

Where there is an environment where Kingdom partnerships (connector); helping others (guide); world relevance (preparer); gift-based vision (inviter) and innovative ministry (confirmer) is taking place, new breed leaders will prosper -- leaders like Mark, who need encouragement and freedom to initiate their leadership identity. When leaders like Mark flourish, every church and ministry will thrive.

Mark found himself in a Kingdom ecosystem through his relationships and opportunities. Now, Mark has transformed his business into a Kingdom ecosystem by providing opportunities for his employees to give and involve themselves in the problems of this world.

Another Kingdom ecosystem example is the Catalyst group, a network of churches in the northern suburbs of Chicago. These congregations, under the banner of "Many communities, One Church," have come together not to adopt common doctrinal statements or to merely fellowship, but to make a difference in their piece of the world.

One of many community outreaches implemented by Catalyst has been its summer, month-long service projects.

Along with helping feed the hungry, offering credit, family and other counseling and a variety of other services, Catalyst has created the ecosystem for participating youth pastors to blossom into this new breed of leader. They've experience the voice of connection, invitation, confirmation etc, and are now influencing other youth leaders in the same way.

You cannot recruit this new breed of leader, but you can create a living, vibrant, global ecosystem where those God-given traits will rise up that will influence others in their spheres of life. In doing so, you will also create a place where believers in Christ will quickly grow to being Christ-centered in their life and calling.

♦ Paul: LIFE is more than church

Paul De Jong is the senior pastor of LIFE in Auckland, New Zealand. He is a strong and effective leader in the classic sense. LIFE has a great vision, a faith-filled strategy and Paul has an incredible capacity to envision others to this calling.

But Paul is also a new breed of leader. He has created a Kingdom ecosystem where Christians are inspired and released to discover and develop their cause in this world.

LIFE is full of people from every corner of the world.

Diverse generations worship and serve together. At LIFE there is a place for the radically unsaved to the sold-out, Christ-centered believer.

Paul cares very much for the church that God has put under his stewardship. Yet Paul also recognizes that LIFE is part of a much larger Kingdom. LIFE invests time, energy and resource into helping other churches and leaders, often at great sacrifice of their own vision. LIFE is an integral part of its community, leading its world.

Nowhere in LIFE's materials (website, brochures, welcome information, etc.) will you see the word church, for Paul – as a new breed of leader – knows that LIFE means far more than church. LIFE is a global Kingdom ecosystem where new breed of leaders flourish and influence many more to join God's cause in this world. LIFE is more than church. That's also probably why it's the largest church in New Zealand.

♦ Back to John the Baptist

It all comes back to the kind of Kingdom leadership epitomized by John the Baptist, whose unique voice is needed again for the spiritual wilderness that encompasses both our global village and the Christians who inhabit the village. We need more friends of the bridegroom, devoted to Him and His Church more than fulfilling particular tasks or living up to the traditional expectations of title. We need a new breed of leader who takes responsibility for everything and for everyone.

Consider Luke 3:1-2 introduction of John: "Now in the fifteenth year of the reign of Tiberius Caesar, Pontius Pilate being governor of Judaea, and Herod being tetrarch of Galilee, and his brother Philip tetrarch of Iturea and of the region of Trachonitis, and Lysanias the tetrarch of Abilene, Annas and Caiaphas being the high priests, the word of God came unto John the son of Zacharias in the wilderness."

At first glance, this passage does not seem to be all that spiritual, does it? Maybe it does not even strike you as inspiring. But consider the historical context: God is coming to Earth.

Who will be the planet's emissary to welcome the King of the Universe? Who, among Earth's leaders, is qualified for such an awesome task?

Well, it was not to be anyone from the established Jewish priesthood of the time. It was o't King Herod, the Romans' puppet, and it was not even Caesar, ruler of the known world and a man who even dared grasp status as a deity for himself. No, none of them would do. It was John, the friend of the bridegroom, who had the voice chosen to prepare the world for its coming Messiah.

Scripture tells it to us simply: "The word of God came to John . ."

Who dares to speak on behalf of God today to the 2 billion believers that serve as God's one and only plan for redeeming His world? Will he have the attitude of John, that in his life and work Christ "must increase, but I must decrease"? John, looking like no other spiritual leader, cared for all who came, whether those he dipped in the Jordan wore designer sandals or came to him with rough, calloused and dusty bare feet. He was unaffected with rank and title.

Referring to his own relationship with the Messiah, John said with brutal honesty that he was not worthy to even loosen his Master's sandal straps. No self-agenda there.

John kept his Kingdom perspective uppermost in his mind, and that kept his voice as a leader pure and crystal clear.

Two thousand years later, it is time again for us to do the same.

ABOUT THE AUTHOR

Joel Holm is a life-long learner and a strategic thinker who has always wanted to make the world a better place. Motivated by his faith, Joel has a passion to help corporations, churches and civic organizations make a genuine, long-lasting impact through creative entrepreneurial initiatives. Joel's recent book, See Life Different, has helped many people gain a fresh, hope-filled view of life. His second book Kingdom Called: Harnessing the Power of Business to Change the World, is influencing business leaders worldwide. Joel has written numerous other books, traveled to more than 90 countries, and studied countless models of business, charity and everything in between. From his vast and unique experiences, Joel brings a wealth of insight and learning to every forum in which he speaks and leads. For more information please contact Joel at joel@joelholm.com